TERRESTRIALS

TERRESTRIALS

Eric Nelson

Texas Review Press
Huntsville, Texas

FIRST EDITION, 2004

Requests for permission to reproduce material from this work should be
sent to:

>   Permissions
>   *Texas Review* Press
>   English Department
>   Sam Houston State University
>   Huntsville, TX 77341-2146

My sincere thanks go to the editors of the magazines in which these
poems, some in slightly different versions, first appeared:

*Alkali Flats, Arts & Letters, Atlanta Review, Bellevue Literary Review, Blue
Moon Review, Carriage House Review, Center: A Journal of the Literary Arts,
Chiron Review, The Christian Science Monitor, The Evansville Review, Free
Verse, Georgia Journal, Laurel Review, Mockingbird, Poetry, Slow Dancer,
Southern Poetry Review, The Southern Review, The Texas Review, Yankee*

"Rockets" first appeared in *The Emily Dickinson Award Anthology, 1999*
"The Flying Map" first appeared in *Proposing On The Brooklyn Bridge:
Poems About Marriage*

I also wish to thank The Hambidge Center for the residencies which
provided time and space for the completion of many of these poems.

**Cover photograph courtesy of Jimmy Westlake: Nine-minute
exposure of 2001 Perseid meteor shower.**

Cover design by Paul Ruffin

Library of Congress Cataloging-in-Publication Data

Nelson, Eric, 1952-
  Terrestrials / Eric Nelson.— 1st ed.
    p. cm.
  ISBN 1-881515-65-6 (alk. paper)
  1. Southern States—Poetry. I. Title.
  PS3564.E4615T47 2004
  811'.54—dc22

                                                    2004002854

For Stephanie

love is love's only destination

CONTENTS

I.

The Garden of Emma

II.

III.

IV.

I

The Garden of Emma

The Walk

My mother believed more in the truths of this world
than anyone I've known—God, Christ, Holy Ghost—
three pies in the sky to her. The day she heard
the story of Jesus' walk upon the water
she walked home and told her grieving mother
she didn't believe it and wasn't going back
to any place that did. She was seven
and already had lost her brother and father.
Between their house and the Delaware River
stood nothing but a dirt road and the weather.
She knew the truth of days of rain, the water
rising and rising. She knew the bitter
facts of sinking and floating, knew better
than to believe anyone walked over, ever.

Justice

When I shot our dog my mother came out of the house
so fast she must have been watching to see
if I'd keep my promise not to shoot a living thing.
She jerked the gun away and stared me down.
It doesn't hurt. It's just a BB gun,
I said. I called the dog and he came, slowly.
She raised the barrel's weight. *Start running,*
she said. Pleading was pointless, so I ran.
I got ten steps before it stung my behind.
I wouldn't cry, but as she, the dog, and the gun
disappeared into the house, everything went
shadowy and blurred, as if I were going blind.
The house itself began to recede, and then
I blinked, the blinds opened, and our eyes met.

Truth

She meets me at the door and sniffs my clothes,
gets face to face and peers into my eyes,
dogs me to the kitchen demanding to know
where I've been, who with, if I've been trying
marijuana, don't lie to her, she's been
to the parents' meetings at the high school
and knows the smell, what to look for, she's seen
a film that shows what smoking pot leads to.
I pull out the kaiser rolls and deli meats,
the mayo, lettuce, onion, tomato
and build a sandwich the size of a hat
while she keeps pressing and smelling me
until I say yes, I've been out smoking dope.
She hugs me hard, says *Oh, don't tell me that.*

Beauty

Faithless, she placed her faith in human works—
the hand-made, handed-down, forgotten, lost
and found in yard sales, flea markets, junk shops.
With missionary zeal, apostle's urge
she saved from ashes and dust the world:
postcards from nowhere to no one you'd know,
a different hand on all of them, the same note—
having, wish, soon, love. Years of calendars
she bought not for the prints but for prints
of another kind—the starred and circled dates,
memorable days in the days of the unremembered—
births and recitals, funerals and dentists.
Turning the months and years of ghosts like gates,
she'd nod, pause, pass on without judgment.

Estate Sale

In my mother's house were many houses.
The garage, the driveway, the yard overflowed
with her relics; two clotheslines hung low,
seven rented banquet tables stretched out.
In cars, on bikes, by foot they came, a crowd
of hagglers and bargain hunters, their voices
slashing the morning air, their money as cold
as their hands as they asked and offered.
They touched the hem of her garments; they knelt
beside boxes with their heads down; they rose
up and reached for the highest of shelves.
They tried on her hats, her jewelry, her shoes.
When they left they left with their glad arms filled
with the spirit and things she saved from this world.

The Remains

Late in the day, nearly everything sold,
two young men appeared, one sickly thin,
a tint of bruises shadowing his skin.
Like prospectors panning a stream for gold,
they sifted the remains as if they might hold
something precious overlooked by everyone.
Though anything of any worth was gone,
they stayed and searched until the air grew cold.
As they left they noticed, under a table,
her old bowling bag, shapeless as a puddle.
The healthy one reached in, pulled out the ball
and laughing, held it for his friend who gazed
as if he were looking into it, the future
before his eyes where her name was engraved.

The Garden of Emma

I hated her those days she had me out
digging holes as round as they were deep,
then filling them again with shrubs and trees.
I hated lugging bags of mulch around
the yard, spreading it carefully into mounds.
I hate nature, I grumbled once, weeding
a bed so rank with hot manure it steamed.
It doesn't care what you think, she said.
You know how this ends—these days I care
for my own yard, devoted as a convert.
I saved her gardening books, not for knowledge
but for the margins where she wrote herself
notes in her florid hand, landscaping plans
that I, against my will, carried out.

Earth Day

Free for the taking on Earth Day
at the Botany Park—spindly,
pot-bound magnolias with few leaves
more alive than dead.
But both kids had to have one,
no matter what I said.

At home I broke the ground
and the kids shoveled
the holes deep enough
for a tree or a child to fit.
They hunkered in, their heads
below the mounds of dirt.
I smiled, but when they wouldn't
get out and began to pull
the dirt in over themselves,
I yanked them up
begrimed as roots.

The younger one welled
with tears, the elder turned
his back as I tore away
the plastic pots, dropped
the saplings in the holes
and buried them.

That night, after baths and dinner
and edgy silences, I went outside
to water. In the dark, I tried
to imagine them grown,
their limbs and leaves, flowers
white and sweet, shade and shadows
falling across the house
like echoes of voices.

Saving Losses

I tell her after she was born
I kept her in my pocket
like a watch
so I couldn't lose her.
She used to believe it,
but she's six and suspicious
now, so she presses her palm
against my palm
and sees her hand more mirror
than miniature, proof
enough that I lie.
I say she's grown a lot,
but she shakes her head
so insistently
I know I've lost.

Triumphant, she grins
like the jack-o-lantern
softening on our porch.
I grin back, thinking
of her lost teeth
gleaming like diamonds
in the felt pouch
behind my socks
in the bureau drawer
where I save them.

In Memory of Money

The unexpected check I got
from his will had little to do
with anything between us.
He wasn't my mother's real father,
and over thirty-odd years
I saw him maybe a dozen times.
The first few I can't remember,
the last few he couldn't.

A penny for my every memory
of him wouldn't fill a wrapper—
white, Woody Woodpecker hair,
smoky teeth, the way he sat
in his chair like Lincoln.
He was the tallest, oldest man I knew.

Whatever I was to him is buried,
a life's savings
inside a jar beneath the floor.

The first money I made
I made shining his shoes.
Unsure about soles,
I polished them, too.
What he thought when he saw
two black shoe prints
staining the rug beside the door
I'll never know.

What he said was
they gave the house a cozy look,
like somebody was always home.

Fitting

Uncle Steve, in memory

No motor could baffle him long,
no broken thing remain unfixed
in his hands, massive as tongs,
etched as stained glass.
No part was unworthy —
bent spokes, sprung levers,
old hoses, flywheels —
all things mechanical
he saved, rigged, set running.

Rigid as a commandment,
fragile as a window,
he couldn't abide
the wrenchings of love,
the turns and counter turns
of hearts, the hurts
families visit on each other.
He could forgive nothing
and lived alone, disconnected
as his telephone.

Mowing his lawn, wrapped
in the engine's tune, his heart
choked and he eased
himself into the grass.
Behind him — green scent
and perfectly even rows.
Before him — the uncut
yard spreading
to the horizon, ragged
growth he'd never get to.

What Anyone Could Do

My father hated onions.
He couldn't stand the stink
and they gagged him once,
his throat closing on the slivers
my mother hid in a casserole
hoping to show him
that what he didn't know
wouldn't hurt him.

Try new things my mother told me.
Tell 'em nothin'
was my father's motto.

The night I spent with Doug,
first friend I saw naked
who was as curious as I,
we lay in his bed tasting each other,
guilt smothered by desire.

The next day my father
asked what we had done.
I said nothing, remembering
dinner when they passed a plate
piled with blinding slices of onion.
All of them, even his little sister
slid some onto their hamburgers.

Not even manners could make me take one.
Watching them chewing, smiling
as they swallowed, I knew
I would never know what anyone,
even I, could do.

Turtles

My father brought me turtles—
box ones it took two hands to hold,
the dark shells drab as a uniform
until I put them down and backed away.
Then the life sprouted, legs
and head emerging like roots.
And then the steady trudge,
as if picking up where they left off,
as if they knew where they were headed.

They always got away—
when I wasn't looking, forgot,
got lost in somewhere else.
They found the weak link,
the loose soil, the tunnel.
I don't remember how many I had,
if I named them, what I fed
or where I kept them.

What's clear now is my father
headed home through the empty
stretches of Texas, loosening his tie
when he sees one poised on the shoulder.
He stops, steps into the rippling,
mirage-like heat and picks it up.
He puts it on the floor, covers it
with his hat and starts up again,
imagining his son's surprise.

Family in the River

Knee-deep or deeper in yellow waders
they fan out into the current —
father and mother, two boys
identical except at the neck
one wears a red and one a blue bandanna,
and a little girl, slim as a minnow.

Quiet as strangers they cast and reel,
separately absorbed at separate angles.

They toss the keepers to the bank.
The girl, stationed in the shallows,
shadowed by an overhanging limb,
waits until their thrashing ends
and carries them to the bucket
wedged between two rocks.

At the horizon, the sky turns
the color of the river, as if the river,
like a treadmill, were coming back,
a belt of slate-colored clouds closing in.

As the girl bends to a fish,
one of the boys tosses another.
It slaps her cheek and flops into the water.
With her yelp the father jerks
around in time to see the splash.
He stares at the spot until it calms,

and then at all, or none of them,
he shouts, *Goddamn this ain't no picnic.*
Nearly to his waist in river, he raises his fist,
then lowers it and turns his back.

The brothers frown at each other, the mother
jigs her line and over her shoulder
watches her daughter crying,
rubbing the red into her face.

The air goes chill.
Tree limbs begin to sway.
Goose-bumps ripple the water.

They look at the darkness
pushing toward them.
The father smiles, shrugs,
and they smile back, as if the punch-line
of some joke they all know
has arrived.

Reeling in, they wade backwards
toward the shore, steadily
closing the distance between themselves
until the sky crazes with lightning
and they stop, petrified in semi-circle
like the last pillars of an ancient temple.

II

Rising and Falling

The roofers on the church
kneel against the pitch,
their hands raining nails.

All morning like bells
their whoops and laughter
echo their hammer blows.

Steeped in heat, their bodies
burned silent by afternoon,
they straddle the vertex and rest.

All of them baptized in stories
of terrible falls, all of them
witnesses, they brace themselves

against the steeple; now they believe
in rafters not rapture, in roofs
sealed with blinding flashing.

Rockets

for my son

He rises through rockets—
models of desire
he crafts and launches
in a spear of hiss and smoke
a needle threading heaven—
a vision of himself
slipping through its eye.

The distance to that
moment is devotion
to angles—fin to engine,
nosecone to fin—
grounding
in the inescapable
laws of drag and thrust,
the bloody art of razors,
cement's fine print,
the indifference of wind.

As if he's breathed
ether, he's giddy
with the invisible, the brief
and timeless pinnacle
before the parachute issues
and he staggers
under the scorched,
sulphurous body
as it drifts down, growing
into his outstretched arms.

The Terminal

Surely these are gods of the body—
three males, three females, all lean and leggy
lounging in their careless beauty
at the airport, waiting to fly
to another runway where they will glide
through footlights in fashions
only they are fit for while we
sit in the dark looking up to them.

Even here, in the equalizing glare
and immensity of the terminal, the mass
distraction of baggage and connections,
even in their mortal dress—
jeans and sweaters, shirts half untucked,
thumbing magazines or napping,
they are spotted—every traveler slows
to stare, stunned by these forms
radiant as Jesus aglow
in the plate glass of a skyscraper.

Gorgeous beyond sexuality, no more erotic
than a violin—its hollow polish
holding silence beautifully—
their bodies still the spirit's
haunting music, for now
we forget that they will grow rich
in crease and tic, in excess skin.
They will see their vision blur,
feel muscle sag, hear the volume
of the world fade, turned down
by some more powerful hand.
Not gods at all, but messengers
bringing ambiguous news
they are condemned to, we turn
to them anxiously, momentarily
staying our impatience to fly.

Herons

To lose some heaviness—spirit and flesh—each day
I walk the path around the park pond.
Two herons—one blue, one white—seem to wait,
the blue on the blue water's edge, camouflaged,
as slim as the cattails surrounding it,
its powdery, matte finish matching the air.
The white one, perched on the splintery bridge,
stands like a sentry, rigid as a spear.

Before I look for them, they see me, watch me lumber
toward them until I think they'll stay. Then they break,
unfold so awkwardly I don't like to see under
the wings, the bones grinding to lift their weight
free of gravity, the dangling useless legs
just clearing the pines marked with survey flags.

Man of Letters

A teacher before I was born, to afford
his family my father joined the Air Force.
He'd shed his uniform as soon as he got home—
no white glove inspections, no dinner
table debriefings, no drills
on military time, none of the things
my friends complained about
and I secretly envied.

When I started snapping *yes, sir*
and *no, sir* and *I don't know, sir*,
the way they did to their fathers,
he told me not to call him that.

I watched him sink
into his easy chair to write his letters.
A box of blue paper in his lap,
the gooseneck lamp beside him
glowing gold, he filled pages
with loops and scrolls
that looked like lines of birds in flight.

The Dream Reels

Returning to the classical family he'd fled,
Jack Nicholson in *Five Easy Pieces* with cross-eyed
Karen Black and the two lesbians they've picked up
tries to get an omelet with toast instead of tomato
and the rigid waitress keeps saying no substitutions,
no side orders, no she doesn't make the rules.

Just before she kicks them out and he slaps
all the dishes off the table, he tells her what to do:

Make a toasted chicken sandwich, he says.
Hold the lettuce, butter, and mayo.
Now hold the chicken.
Bring me the toast and a bill for the sandwich
and you haven't broken any rules.

Hold the chicken, she sneers.

Yeah, he says calmly, *hold it between your knees*.

From the time I first saw it when I was 20
and wore my unwashed hair and clothes like a uniform,
that scene has been my guide to all I did
and didn't want to be.

I keep it on the trophy shelf
inside my head, beside the dream reels in which
I punch Steve Gilbert in the face for calling me a Jew,
and I don't apologize to Mrs. Salem for snorting
when she declares *Love Story* a classic,
and I don't let my parents talk me out of coming home
with my black girlfriend because of the neighbors,
and I tell a client to fuck himself when he says
he'll fire me if I can't play hardball.

It's the scene I forget when I remember
what bills are due, which faces
I'll see tomorrow, where my regrets are hidden.

Last night, trash at the curb for tomorrow's pickup,
kids asleep, wife in bed reading,
dogs on the couch—one snoring
and one farting—I was thrilled
again by Nicholson's cool, lethal gaze,
his deliberate words, his perfect timing.

I grinned with the chain-smoking, filth-hating
lesbian's spiky praise from the back seat,
telling Jack how *fantastic* he'd been, how cleverly
he'd figured how to get his toast.

His answer—a throwaway lost in road noise
and the camera's eye on the woman's face—
thundered when one of the dogs
rolled over the remote:

Yeah?
Well I didn't get it, did I?

Then the camera settles on the road
making its steep climb into the mountains
where Jack will kneel before his dying father
and try, through his tears, to explain himself.

The Looters

Escaped, they are captured,
framed on the front page.
A shattered storefront gapes
behind two girls fleeing,
arms piled to their chins with dresses.
All grins and heads thrown back,
they look for all the world
like Wheel-Of-Fortune winners.

The part of me that subscribes
to the news and saves my kids'
teeth wants what they take
to be meat, medicine, cake—
wants their faces struck
with dignity and rage.

The part surrounded
by smoke and smoulder,
a felled forest where bulldozers
churn chevron tracks—
says *Run, run faster,*
escape into those dresses,
turn before mirrors like models
and see how necessary
and beautiful you are.

Recovery

Mending itself like a misused lover, the body
I've longed to escape for the sake of my soul's rise
through green to blue to holiness, lies in its great, dumb ache.

Guilty and free as the one who ends an affair, I look
past pain and drift away from the body's calls
like the calls of the poor, the homeless, the crazed.

The body shifts, presses the scar that runs like a grin
from hip to scrotum, presses down and rises, crashes
into the woods, lumbers on all fours through underbrush,

over roots and rot and fallen, snake-riddled limbs,
follows the sound of a stream, guzzles greedily, swats gnats
between its legs, moves unaware of thorn stabs,

lies in the sun in a drowse until the scent of death leads it
to the carcass of a deer, the slick guts spilled, the vacant eye
looking up, the stink gathering strength, beckoning the body

to lie down and roll in it, to absorb what it has always known.
Waking from a dream of wings, I see in the window a face—
dirt-smeared, bloody, familiar—looking down on me.

The Reptile House

A mid-winter, midnight tour, we walked
through the humid, cave dark room, our only light
red-filtered lamps to best observe but not

disturb the lidless eyes, the dead-white
bellies that rose like vapor on the glass
until they stood a moment upright

then fell gracelessly into the fake grass
writhing and tonguing and rising once more.
It seemed we shouldn't be there, a trespass—

like spying through the crack of a door
someone rising dripping from a bath, or one
struck down by grief sobbing on the floor.

At last we reached the end where we'd begun.
Outside, in the icy, starlit night we couldn't see
but sensed, above the clouds rising from our lungs,

something looming, hidden in the trees—
dark shapes with spear-shaped tails and wings,
peacocks larger than men watching us freeze.

A Mind of Summer

Though the heat keeps me sleepless, I resist
the air-conditioner, preferring the feel of outside.
A likeness of myself moistens the sheets.

Listening to nothing—all sound
smothered in air too heavy to carry
even the smallest vibration—I imagine

papery wings fanning a breeze,
snakes lengthening along the coolest surface
they can find, a deer shifting

its weight, licking a humid leaf.
Then something, maybe the weight of heat
itself, sets a dog off, a long, slow,

echoing wail disappearing like a vapor
trail, then starting again as the last wisp
of sound fades. Over and over. Like a word

repeated so many times it becomes pure,
the dog's voice becomes the sound of being
alone and knowing it for the first time,

like the alley I walked past last winter,
the day a color between coal and smoke,
when I saw a pair of legs disappear up the black

steps of a fire-escape, and a woman leaning out
a window below, calling, over and over, a name
I couldn't make out, but the sound hollow,

empty of anything but itself calling itself.
I couldn't stand it and walked on, the voice
becoming my own voice calling my own name.

I can't stand it now. I go outside and look
into the darkness and silence
for the vague shape of a dog.

It must have run when it heard the door.
Back in bed, I wait for it to start
again, and think a few times that it has,

but it is only my mind doing tricks,
rolling over, fetching its own stick,
chasing its inescapable tail.

Stilts

When her life is nearly more
than she can bear—boring,
inscrutable, beyond her
eight-year-old's control—
she gets the stilts she got
for Christmas and rises up
and walks away, above it all,
tall strider, kind giant
high-stepping down
the driveway to the sidewalk
and around the block,
the neighborhood dogs
wagging behind fences,
paws to the top
of chain-link, necks stretched
for the sky, barking
their owners up and out
to hush them and wave
to the one girl parade,
the tall ship all sail
and mast across the tips
of evergreens, body and spirit
for once not at odds, for now
everyone lifted up with her.

Tibet Yet Here

South Georgia's a world from Tibet, yet here
they are, eight exiled monks in their buzz cuts
and flowy red robes in the middle of the union
making a mandala for peace. Surrounded
by the odor of french-fries and carpet shampoo,
the richochet of game room and students
in backward hats and bags festooned with buttons,
they bow to their work, bending over a table
to tap fine, brightly dyed sand–blue, yellow, red, green
from funnels as thin as birds' beaks into intricate geometry.

They work in shifts, four at a time in that backbreaking pose,
stopping only for the food court buffet where they load up
on greens and fried chicken, beets and blueberry crumble.
They eat and chatter and laugh and fill their plates again.
From a makeshift gift shop they sell jewelry and incense,
Free Tibet t-shirts and stickers. None of them speak much
English, but they gladly take credit cards
and handle the machine like pros.

When they finish, the gorgeous sphere shines
like a planet everyone hoped for but can't believe.
Before anyone becomes attached, the monks pull out small
brooms and sweep the sand into a plain brown box.
Chanting a chant that floats like the call of an ancient bird,
the monks lead a small crowd to Eagle Creek,
a drainage ditch from which the football team
takes ironic inspiration. After a short prayer, the monks shake
the glittering sand onto the surface of the slow current
where it trembles like a fallen rainbow.

As the crowd drifts off, a small boy runs back, dips his hands
into the creek, raises them like wings above his head
and shouts something that nobody understands.
Everyone looks from the boy to the monks, fearing an offense

if not a sacrilege. Their robes flickering in the sunset,
the monks wave to the boy, water spilling through his fingers,
his hands gloved in the brilliant grains of sand.

III

Art of the Middle Ages

The faces of angels and cherubs don't move,
hovering as they do above it all,
their smooth, sweet features radiant
and vacant, their bodies lost in clouds.
No comfort waits in their wings, no home
behind their dark, sparkling eyes.
The faces that draw me
are worn, weighed down with gravity and time,
engraved with the strangeness of living—
laugh lines seared so deep
they look like scars, foreheads creased
as if branded, necks ringed by wrinkles
like age-rings in a tree.
Splotched, spotted, withered, enflamed—
from such faces love has poured out
and been withheld, anger absorbed
and vented, sorrow pinched and deflected.
Every human hope and doubt has left
a trace, as when a stream, evaporating,
rising to nothing, leaves behind its bed,
cracked and boned, its depths revealed at last.

By Fire

When I was twelve I climbed
our roof at night to be alone.
I didn't know what life to live—
the one beneath me with the lights on,
everyone happy one minute
and crying the next,
or the one up there, invisible
but constant, more certain than my body.
Half the time I watched the sky,
the stars, the space between
until I seemed to float, evaporate
into pure, uncomplicated air.
Then I turned and watched my street
like God, puzzled and absorbed:
a man leaning on his car, singing
to himself, then stopping
to bring his armpit to his nose;
a woman in front of her open
refrigerator, staring into it,
rubbing between her legs;
a porch light flicking on, a girl
older than me stepping out
in her nightgown calling
Bootsy, Bootsy.

One night an edge of sky began
to glow like sunrise.
I must have waited for an hour
for it to turn into a gauzy
human form, beckoning.
I listened for a voice like the voice
that called from the burning bush.
Nothing happened, but the sign
had come, I knew, and I came down

like Moses, cleansed and clarified.
Next day I learned that what I'd seen
was the most expensive restaurant
in the city going up in flames.
While I had watched, inspired,
two dozen people discovered
that there was no escape
and burned or jumped to death.

On television, the survivors
thanked God for watching over them.
I burned for them, and God,
but mostly for myself.
I want to say I never climbed
the roof again, hoped for God again.
But I was twelve and still believed
what I believed wasn't in my head.
More and more, though, I looked down,
looked forward to the girl
in the nightgown calling her dog
and hugging it when it appeared
in the apron of porch light.

Boys and Nature

for David Graham

In steady rain a boy maybe ten,
his soaked shirt sagging like old skin,
took off his belt and whipped a small tree
steadily, without heat, as if it were his job.
As I watched, mystified, from my office,
a day from my own mysterious boyhood returned.

Intent in my garage, I filled a cardboard box
with bugs and grass and put a match to them,
forgetting boxes flame as well as insects.
Whatever fascination I felt
watching caterpillars writhe and crisp
disappeared when the walls blistered and caught.
I ran to the house, assumed a face
as calm as those around me, planning
my surprise when the fire trucks arrived.

Given the right amount of rain and a tree
so self-contained, I too might have whipped it,
my will at war with forces I couldn't grasp.
It wasn't tree or rain, bugs or fire,
but something inside we were beginning
to know we didn't want to know,
that needed beating back or burning down.

My sister saw the smoke, squelched the fire
and kept it from my parents.
The boy gave up at last and walked away,
swinging his belt in front of him.
The tree held up its green umbrella.
The rain went on for days.

Terrestrials

When God wouldn't talk, I turned
to UFOs, hovering in the airwaves
those days of Cuban missiles
and stockpiles of canned goods.
One greater being was as good
as another, any shape the sky held—
ladder or halo, saucer or cigar—
miracle enough in my temporary world
of transfers and states of alert.

In the library of the Air
War College where my father studied,
I prowled the stacks for the Blue Books
that confirmed sightings and contacts.
I never found them; I found lies—
tricked-up frisbees, weather balloons,
and rows of decades-old issues of *Life*
bound in books the size of clay tablets.

I sat on the floor and stared
at the gray images—piles of dead,
naked bodies; men in baggy suits
and hats that hid their eyes;
women with iron hair and dresses
like uniforms; skeletons of buildings;
a sailor kissing a nurse.
I lost time as the years that led
from them to me passed through my hands
and into my skin like dust.

A tingling started in my legs
and rose through my body.
I stood up, dizzy, surrounded
by the pictures spread out below me

like an aerial map of the world.
I stood still, waiting
for the spinning to stop.

Pearls

The summer we were best friends, Bobby Howeter and I
snuck out every week through the shadows
and the streetlight hum of our sleeping town.
We disappeared into the blind fairways of the golf course,
took off our clothes and waded into the lake muck
feeling with our toes for the hard curves of golf balls.
We barely spoke. We listened to the ripples our bodies made.
We lobbed the balls onto the close grass of the near
green until there were enough to fill two grocery bags.
The next day we'd wait at the twelfth tee and sell them
to golfers–four for a dollar, three if they were Titleists.
We spent most of it at the swimming pool snack bar.
Who knows where the rest went.

One night near summer's end, on our way home, I wanted to go
past Bridgette's house, the girl whose French mother
had all the other mothers talking. What she wore. What she said.
Bridgette came to the pool alone and didn't look for anyone.
Didn't watch when Bobby and I played *Pearls Before Pirates*,
in which we dove for a golf ball at the bottom of the deep end.
Bobby didn't want to—we weren't sure where she lived,
the bags were heavy, and why, was what he wanted to know.

When we finally stood on the sidewalk at her house,
he asked me if I liked her. He was just asking.
But it made me want to get away from him.
As I turned, the bottom of my bag dropped out and the balls
bounced off the concrete like hail into Bridgette's yard.
Bobby's bag landed with a dead-body thud and we ran.
We ran until we fell, laughing, rolling on the grass,
crawling on all fours, wiping drool from our mouths.
We laughed, imagining Bridgette in the morning
looking at her yard scattered with golf balls. Like pearls,
I thought. "Like eggs," Bobby hooted, offering his hand.

The Promise

We filled our mouths with each other,
took into our hands our tenderest buttons,
left stains on our parents' couches, carpets, cars.
Like incense we inhaled the smell
of sex, our frankincense and myrrh.
Sometimes, after, I'd feel something
like guilt, and teen-age poet that I was, I wrote:
I've hung my balls like mistletoe.
One night after hours
of fogging the car, as we composed ourselves,
she found the zipper of her dress broken beyond hope.
Driving to her house, I promised God
I was his if he'd get us out of this.
Her father met us at the door.
I stood behind her trying not to look
at the fissure, the chasm of her naked back.
He grumbled and went to bed.
She ran for her room and I for my car.
The next night we were back, frantic
to enter each other's skin.
Her hand inside my pants, my tongue inside her mouth,
I remembered the promise I made
and shuddered with release.

Prisoners at the Park

The before-work joggers gone,
the mothers with strollers not together yet,
the brown-baggers still growling at their desks,
a detail of prisoners

in khakis and orange vests prune hedges,
rake diamonds, pat spring flowers into beds.
Shovels, edgers, shears,
canvas sacks and shoulder slings
lie like game equipment
beside the prison bus, school bus

in another life.
On the bridge across the pond a couple
in bulky clothes press awkwardly together
as if keeping from falling
into the shadowy water. In their shadow
fish gather and turtles nose.

Drifting from the bridge to the parking lot,
their bodies move like bodies waking up,
reluctant to wake up.

A prisoner hoses duck slime from their path.

At the far end of the lot, between the only two cars,
she braces herself against a door.
He fits himself over her, her face inside his coat,
his arms like rope around her.

A guard, leaning on a tree, looks

as if he is looking for his girl to show,
his shotgun at his side.

She twists away and opens
the door, sits in the driver's seat,
rolls the window down and speaks to him.

He leans in, then she is out
and they hold themselves again, sink

between the cars, beneath the blue air

chained with birds
while a line of orange vests
flicker and disappear into the bus.

The Flying Map

The day we drove 200 miles into Virginia
looking for a town we'd heard was filled
with books and antiques we never found
because the town was in Maryland—
how to explain not turning back when we agreed
we didn't know where we were going

except that autumn light
tinted the maples and apples;
and that love is love's only destination.
When we thought to check a map, you opened it
fold by fold across our laps, the blue and red lines
like charged wires between us.

As you lifted it for a closer look,
the wind ripped it out the window
into an origami bird flapping over us.
Of that vivid day most vivid now
is the sound of our unstoppable laughter
as we drove on to nowhere we knew.

Woman Absorbed in an Orange

Turning it in her palms,
she senses the pressure it takes

to peel the thick outer layer
without puncturing the flesh within.

The rind unrolls, reveals
the ball inside the ball, the sphere

she slips her thumbs inside
and divides, whole into halves,

a single glistening bead
sliding to her wrist.

One by one she separates
the perfect crescents and gives them

to her mouth, her lips swelling
with each disappearing,

an aura of orange surrounding her.

Spring Again

In time we all see, with variations, the scene yesterday
in front of an old house turned into apartments.
A woman—dark clothes and young yesterday—walks
away from a frozen man in shorts and spiky hair.

Her stride, his open palms, say something as delicate
as a jeweled watch or a crystal egg has fallen.
Passing in our cars we recognize him and want to
shout   *Stop her   Say something   Move*

When she doesn't look back for traffic but drops
her crossed arms and swerves into the road,
we brake, realize we know her and open our mouths
to say   *Go back   Don't cross   Stop.*

Without a sound our lips close and our throats tighten
though it is spring again and the dogwoods unwrap
one after another their bright, exquisite gifts.
When we look in our rear-views, they are gone.

Gardenias

After the showy floats of forsythia and azalea,
after the nosegays of jasmine and wisteria,
after the beauty queens are uncrowned
and resume their ordinary lives,

gardenias turn their lights on, their first glow
inside the spiral buds spreading
wider and whiter, the unwrapped petals
dense as rising cream, the odor

thickening, more substance than scent, a lotion
laving us, seeping into us, deepening us.
We fill every vase, jar, bottle, glass,
convert every room with them.

Our bed lit dimly with them, our bodies
like gardenias achieve their sweetest,
fullest power as they fade and turn
downward with age.

IV

The Black House

The house in the kitchen frightened him—
the chains against the wall, the cold
weights he was told not to touch,
the sharp, carved wood, black wood,
the black house like a house
in the forest where children are forgotten.

He waited for the first click like a latch,
the second like a step on a cracked stair.
He listened for the white bird to break
out and squawk as if trying to escape
before it vanished, slammed
behind the door.

Triumph

Beginning the moment you fold
your leg like a bird's wing over the saddle
and your wrists rehinge themselves
to clutch brake and throttle
you can't think on a motorcycle

can only be your body alive
every nerve ending open every pore bored out
the world of your five senses funneled through you
the sound of speed not high and thin
but low deep broad roaring both
a river and the tunnel under it both
pressing you to bend to let go to take it all
in one drowning swallow the world a liquid
pouring into and over you a drink a dream
a drained sea a bed of salt
preserving the perishable

flashing before your blurred eyes
the fine green fields the pines the gullies and rills
the broken yellow lines a single line
a coachwhip cracks across and disappears
in the mixed odor of rotting spread-eagled doe
on the shoulder by jasmine
climbing telephone poles and overflowed
dumpsters like sour towels slapped over you
as a red hawk bursts upward from the marsh
beside you the great serrated wings almost clipping
you as they rise and fall like pistons muscling
the air until the hawk breaks the trees and banks
in its talons the mistaken squirrel taken
by its already punctured neck
dangling like the flowers on the makeshift shrines
wedged with stones the crosses
hand painted and wreathed and stuffed with scraps

you imagine the moment of leaving the road
behind you in a burst of last life electrified
with fear and power your body thrown off
into a plowed field beneath a clean slate sky

slowing down to return to the world
rushing back to you
the blur clearing into hard lines
of buildings cars people
moving slowly slower slow
you downshift them into perspective and balance
it all at red lights where the heat, the exhaust, the steel
press against you on the asphalt, the globes
of spit and dripped oil black holes
making you thirst to throttle on into wind
you make and tilt against yourself

Against Green

I love the eyesores that break-up
the relentless green pastures:
the abandoned shacks, barns and sheds
staggered by gravity, weather-shaken, insect-bored.

If not silent as dust, they would cough, sputter, sigh inside
their sinkhole roofs, caved rafters, unplumbed walls.
Slipping like discs, crooked as teeth,
they slump and lean, tremble sooner than a leaf.
Yet they stand; go down, yes, but slowly, one
step at a time. Sometimes just the roof
rises above a green sea, the tin cornice
sparkling like a flare, the collapsed walls drifting like rafts.

Camouflaged, overtaken by vegetation,
shrubs, creepers, vines clinging to them,
still their odd, unnatural shape
humps the landscape.

Yesterday I passed a two-story house, intact
but askew, the columned facade—as much rot
and mildew as wood—
tilting on its axis.
Across the rusted roof, consuming the roof,
wild honeysuckle raged, great tongues of it
hanging from the eaves and licking the windows.
From the chimney, masses of fiery blossoms
erupted and flowed like lava.

The Stubbornness of Farms

Beyond this tract of suburban homes, the farms
lie shrunken now that used to spread themselves
like carpet—wall to wall across our lawns,
peanuts and beans in rows as plumb as the shelves
the builder built in every family room.
The pond our dogs nose out when they get free
quenched a pasture antic with goats and mules.

The farm this sub-division used to be,
invisible behind the stand of pine,
reduced to house and shed and chicken feed,
won't go away, for every afternoon
the last of the mules, stubborn at the fence-line,
blasts its pitiful brays as if to plead
for light to stay, not to be left alone.

The Difficult Name

Every day I stutter through it,
look up for help, a face to claim it.

Not here, not here, not here, not here . . .
the x's add up—
student in name only,
student of parties, of daddy's money,
of sleep and forgetting.

On each revised roll the name remains.
I ignore it and settle in
for the long term.
Then the Registrar's memo arrives—
the student died the day school began.

The name I couldn't pronounce—
two words for nothing now
and never absent.

Without knowing I'm going to,
I whisper it
below the hearing of the class.
My lips push the syllables like stones,
my lungs strain against their cage.
I feel my collar close around my neck
and I look up
as if for an answer.

The Vision Center

Everyone tired, late afternoon,
we slump into cushions until one
by one we rise to our names
and walk the long hall
to take our drops.

Then we are back, sitting still
while our pupils expand, black holes
sucking light into our heads,
all ordinary things growing
sharper, charged—
a chair morphs into more than itself,
an idea embroidered, a form
so perfect it levitates
in its own glow—all borders sizzling
like sparklers, the dullest shape
frizzed with prisms,
the careening light clothing us.

Outside the sun fires flares so piercing
we know it's what the dying see,
what the back-from-the-dead remember
as it gushes from clouds,
a flood sweeping everything into one
brass-bright funnel like a trumpet's bell,
our dark lenses stopping our eyes
from revealing too much.

The Navigator

All shot up, Rum Dum guttered
through clouds as dense as the sea
between you and England
in the only war story you'd tell.

Fuel and altitude needles skipping,
the gunner's belly oozing, the pilot
cursed and doubted the course
you plotted, hunched
over your compass and charts.

You insisted you were right
though you weren't sure
until the plane broke through
and the crew broke out in cheers
at the sheer sight of Dover's cliffs.

Sixty years from them, your head shaved,
skull cut from your bloody brain, you look
shell-shocked and little hope

you know who you were—
course setter, path finder, steady needle
I cursed and followed, doubted and obeyed.

Blank as your expression the sky is
Florida blue and always
cloudless in your hospital window.

In the blindness of an unwatched night
you pull the feeding tube from your stomach

out your nose, yank the IV out,
peel away the monitor and leg wraps,

slip somehow through the bed bars
and stumble for the door you don't see,

out of your clouded head
one word breaking through—*home*.

Which is greater—the sky
or death to navigate?

Your mind skips like a needle
between today and today
of another latitude, a needle
swelling your body into a float
they say will deflate in time.

All I know to do is hope
for the fog you stutter through
to burn off in one swift strike,
dazzling cliffs again
there to confirm you.

Gifts

1.

Wedged deep in the dark heart
of the Christmas tree, hidden
until our strung lights caught it—
the unfallen oval of a bird's nest.

Woven straw and paper, flecked
with red foil, it glinted from within
like embers in wind, like chimes
insisting what is gone is here still.

2.

In winter, the pecan grove off 67
looks like a settlement abandoned—
all whistling wind and slow collapse,
splintered limbs sagging like rafters.

Invisible to winter, foretold in roots,
the paper shells and wreath green leaves
return, every tree a gift
bearing gifts, every emptiness filled.

Elegy for J.D.D. Duncan, Undertaker

I bought his fountain pen, circa 1930's, in an antique town
in West Virginia where he had been the undertaker
over sixty years.

Its quality still shined in the black, translucent celluloid,
the solid gold clip, and the wide as a wedding ring
cap band where his name was engraved.

I imagined it in his breast pocket, the clip
straight as a compass needle, his composure
reassuring the grief-broken, his name in their hands
steadying them when they signed the hard, necessary papers.

At home I flushed the dust and dry ink, filled it
with Waterman's South Sea Blue
and found it wrote with such fluid ease
that it made even my writing graceful, rolling, wave
after wave breaking against the ruled margin.
I thought of him, his life against death, over and over
sealing the leaky bodies
for their long sinking into dirt.

Except for a speck of missing gold, it looks as new
as the day he got it, perhaps as a gift, an emblem
against everything lost, buried, land-locked.

A rhythmic whisper like distant singing
rises from the nib as I write,
and a blue, indelible wake ripples over the surface.

The Badge

I've come to help them win
their creative composition badge.

They're six, seven—what do they know
of loss, writing's source and subject?

So I tell them we lose things
as we get older, and poems help

save them, make pain less painful.
They stare so blankly

they seem not to have heard
much less understood.

Then, slowly, their hands go up.
One at a time they name their losses—

gloves, teeth, bicycles, charms,
dogs, friends, houses, parents—

a roll-call of hurts until all have spoken.
We take up our pencils and begin.

Art

October, a woman and a boy, a tumor
overtaking his brain, draw pictures
in the waiting room.

She makes a red apple as round
as a face. Then from her hand a cloud
grows and darkens over the apple

until the crayon breaks inside
its wrapper and hangs like a snapped
neck from her bloodless fingertips.

He's drawn two stick-figures
up to their necks in falling gold
leaves, their heads all smiles.

It's you and daddy, he tells her.
Above them a flock of m's
fly toward a happy sun.

When she doesn't answer
he says on Halloween he'd like
to be a horse with orange wings.

Staring at his picture, she says
It looks like Thanksgiving.
Where are you?

He taps the sun, *I'm shining on you.*
She hugs him as if trying
to press him back inside her.

I'm not crying, she whispers.
He looks over her shoulder.
I'm not crying, too.

Love Birds

Near the end her body wasn't hers,
she wasn't in it anymore as she lay
in her dressing gown,
cassettes and player beside her,
listening to her music, looking out
at the birds and the lake beyond
as if she were already there.

The year before I started school,
every morning after my father
and sisters left, she'd stack the dishes
and load a stack of 33's inside
the huge hi-fi in the living room.

She'd sing the songs
we both had memorized—
"Some Enchanted Evening,"
"I Could Have Danced All Night,"
"If Ever I Should Leave You"—
her voice rising and fading
through the house while I raced
my cars around the hook rug
in the family room.

For lunch we ate egg or tuna salad.
How eager I was for school,
to carry books and eat in a cafeteria.
After *The Edge of Night* and *The Guiding Light*
brought to us by *Tide*, we'd get a nap
before my sisters got home.

What love birds we were, nestled
in our cage singing—her songs
of love and yearning, my own
desires and imaginings
while the world went on without us.